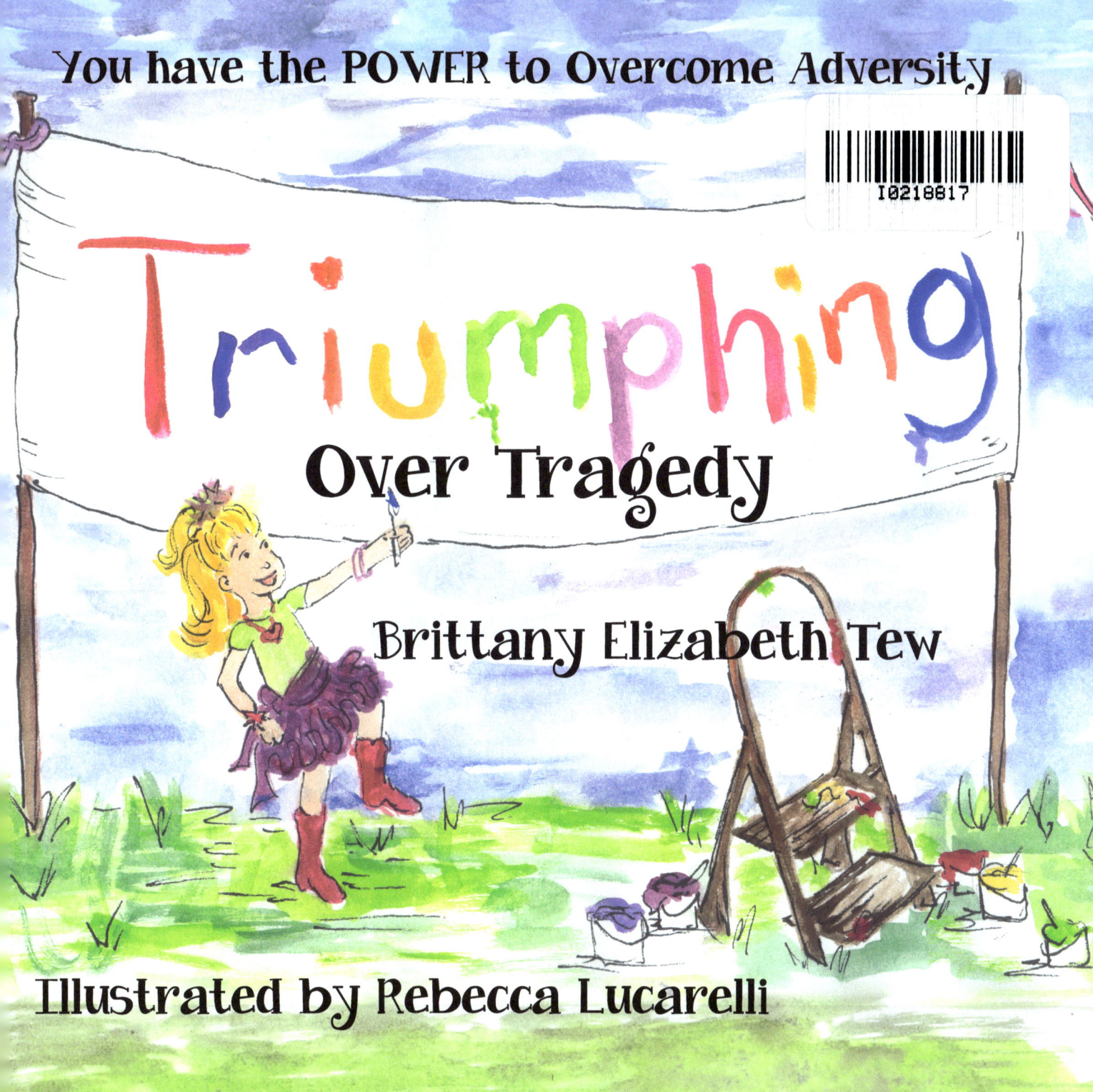

There once was a happy, blonde, little girl,
 Who loved to dance, to sing and to twirl.

She had several sisters that she loved very much;
 They played in dresses, boas, crowns, and such.

One day her family got some very bad news-
Doctors said a sister she would soon lose.

Brittany's littlest sister
was going to die;

How would her family
ever learn to get by?

They loved the baby sister every way every day
And then one day, they were forced to say-
Goodbye and we'll miss you forever and always;
The love in their hearts continues and stays.

Brittany's little heart hurt and happy times were few,
But she learned what to do when she felt blue.

Everyone has struggles sometime in their life-
 Like parents divorcing, pets dying and everyday strife.

She found other people had some hard times too,
 How to get through it? – there must be a clue.

Bad things can happen and sometimes they do
 So what do you do when it happens to you?

Brittany soon learned how to stop being sad-
   She had the POWER to get through all of the bad.

The steps to heal were right in each letter-
   P – O – W – E - R was how Brittany felt better.

"P" is the notion to Press On and keep going-
　　Some days were hard, but she kept on growing.

Don't give up on sad days when you really want to quit;
　　Push on, right when you'd rather just sit in a pit.

Press on means to live each day to the fullest;
　　Living past the pain made the days not the dullest.

Make the best of each day, despite all the pain; Brittany discovered how to dance in the rain!

Overcoming the hard times has a second step- its true
   Focusing on Others was the right thing to do.

One day at school, Brittany saw a friend crying
   Her friend said she was soon moving, and wasn't lying.

Brittany turned her attention from herself to her friend;
She found helping Others helped her own heart to mend.

There really was POWER in giving to Others.
Brittany started seeing her world in brighter colors!

Hard times are just hard, as the name does imply,
Step three is to get past the pitfalls of "Why."

Brittany had questions- she wanted to know "Why"
"Why did her little sister have to just die?"

The more that she pondered the "whys" to obsession
She didn't feel any better nor answer her question.

Focusing on the "whys" will make you go crazy!
    She found it was a waste of time and a way to be lazy.

Looking at "What Now" instead of the "Why"
    Got her re-directed with plans as big as the sky.

The POWER was losing the "Whys" for "What Now"
    Brittany was triumphing over tragedy and she knew how.

The next step in POWER is easy- you just have to share,
By finding an adult who will listen and care.

Know there's POWER in talking strong feelings all out-
<u>E</u>xpressing <u>E</u>motions in good ways
makes you feel better, no doubt.

It is easy to find people to talk to,
who really do care;
Talk to your parents, teachers,
or God with a prayer.

Sometimes it is hard,
'cause you feel all
alone by yourself;
Brittany found lots of people
she could talk to
just by herself.

The "R" in POWER is so important, you will see.
For it stands for "Rise Up" to be all you can be.

For your life is not what you choose,
        but what you've been given;
So make it the best that you can possibly be living!

Hard times make the good times seem so much better,
    So continue to rise up and follow
        POWER with each letter.

In the whole world, there is no one exactly like you;
    Know you are wonderfully made and
        God loves you too.

YOU are the best You,
    so be great and stand tall;
You can overcome tragedy-
    any and all!

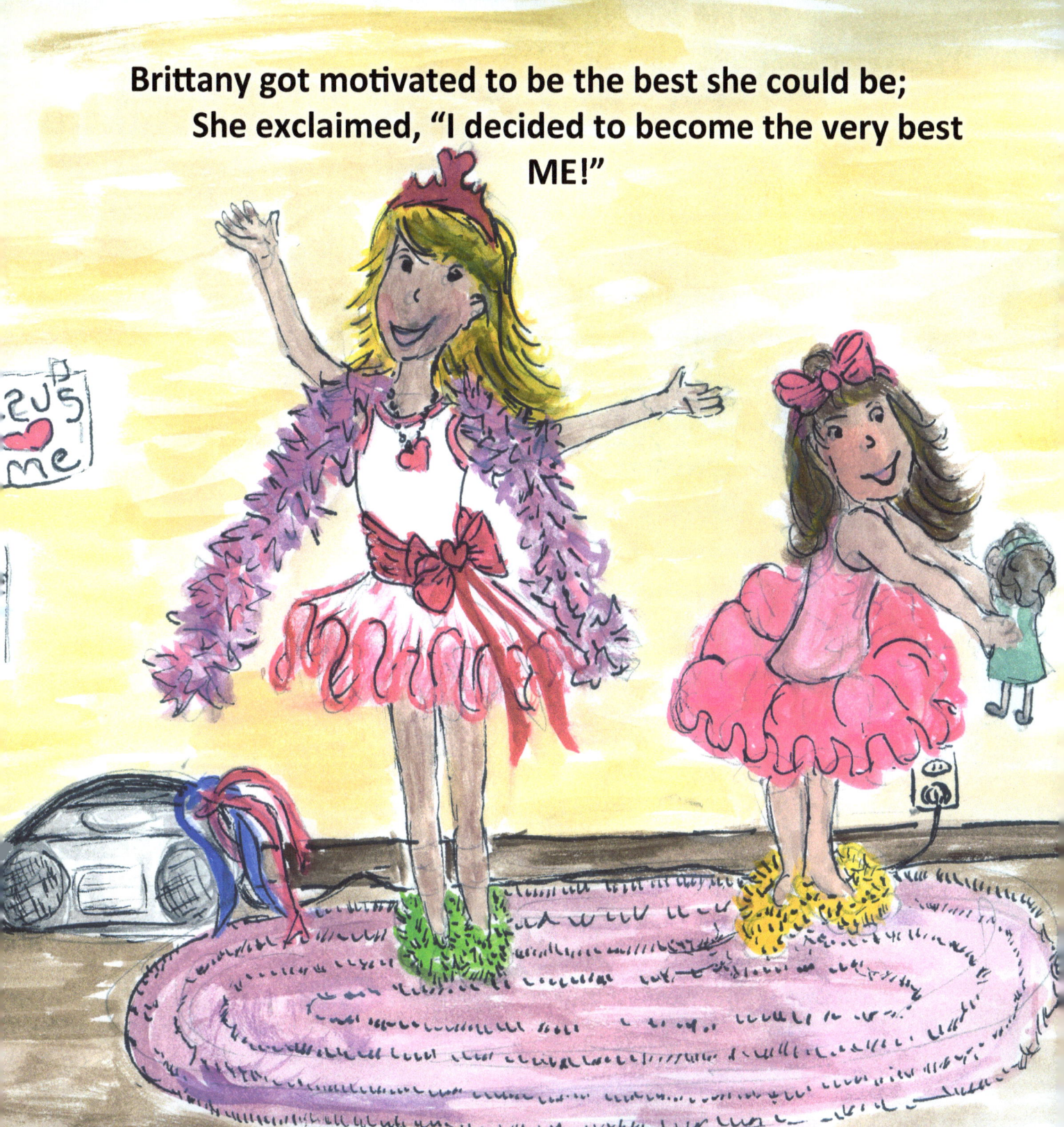

*The Steps of POWER-*

Everyone will be faced with difficulties sometime in his or her life. Adversity in life is a given reality, crossing all gender, socio-economic and racial barriers; so if you are not facing a difficulty, you can know that one is headed your way. But you can triumph through using the acronym POWER. I strive to help others by sharing my story and spreading the message of hope that can help others to rise up and triumph over their own hard times. I have triumphed over tragedy by knowing that I had the power to do so. Power is spelled P-O-W-E-R. The **P** in POWER stands for Press on- to overcome tragedy, one has to keep going, and doing everything to your best ability in order to fulfill their true purpose here on earth. The **O** in Power is for Overcoming tragedy by helping Others. We can feel better ourselves if we make someone else feel better. By sharing life stories, we can aspire to inspire someone else who is facing turmoil in their life. The **W** stands for What now? instead of Why? Sometimes as human beings with limited insight, we get so fixated on "Why did this happen to me?" instead of focusing on the bigger picture. Getting entangled in the web of "why" can make us feel helpless and hopeless. We need to focus on "What will we do now?" in order to overcome the tragedy. The **E** in power stands for Expressing Emotions in a healthy way. Always remember- you're not alone in this time of difficulty! Talk to a parent, counselor, or a trusted adult and share your feelings instead of letting them boil up inside of you, turning you into a bitter person ("Choose to be Better not bitter!"). The **R** in power stands for Rise up to be your best! Be true and kind to yourself because you are wonderful, and there is no one else like you. Live life to its fullest and reach for your greatest potential. I want you to know that YOU have the Power to Triumph over Tragedy!

**Brittany's Story-** Tragedy has been a frequent experience in my life. In 2001, my two-year-old sister, Caroline, died after her two-year long battle with a rare degenerative brain disease. She had a Leukodystrophy (which is a group of disorders that center around problems with the white matter in the brain); her brain began to die and to calcify, which caused her to be blind, deaf, mute, unable to control any part of her body from her neck down, and to make it worse- she had seizures all of the time. Doctors explained that there is no known cause and no known cure for the disease. Despite all of her medical problems, she smiled and laughed every day- what a lesson my family learned from her!! In 2006, my grandfather died of Lou Gehrig's disease; I watched my sweet granddad "DonDon" deteriorate for several years before his passing. In 2008, another one of my four sisters, Alexandria, died after a three and a half year degenerative battle with the same rare brain disease that had taken my sister Caroline, leaving another huge loss in my life. Then in 2009, my ventriloquism coach and role model, Amy Jones, lost her battle with an aggressive form of Renal Cell Carcinoma cancer. My life has been marked with several heart breaking losses, therefore I am passionate about sharing my story of triumph to inspire and impart hope to those facing their own adversity.

I also desire to promote awareness of rare diseases in order to bring about more research and funding to find a cure for these diseases. There are 6,800 disorders that are recognized as "rare diseases" by the National Organization for Rare Disorders (NORD). A disorder is classified as rare when it affects less than 1 percent of the population, like the medical conditions that my sisters died from. By partnering with the United Leukodystrophy Foundation and NORD, I want to educate the public about Leukodystrophies and other rare diseases that affect people like my sisters.

**Donations can be made online to support Rare Disease Research- www.rarediseases.org**
**Donations can be made online to support Leukodystrophy research at www.ulf.org**
**\*Note: A portion of the proceeds from the sale of this book will be given to the ULF.**

## About the Author- Brittany Elizabeth Tew

She is a 16 year-old Honors Student at Carroll High School in Southlake, Texas. Britt is the oldest of 5 daughters of Kristi and Todd Tew. Outside of school, Brittany is an avid reader and writer, plays piano and is an accomplished ventriloquist. She has been a local title holder in the Miss America's Outstanding Teen Organization for several years. She is involved in National Charity League and is a member at First Baptist Church, Dallas. She plans to be a 4th generation Baylor Bear, and wants to become a Pediatrician to help children.

Todd, Kristi, Brittany, Victoria and Caroline in 2001

Brittany, Victoria, Katherine & Alexandria (twins) in 2005

## About the Illustrator- Rebecca Lucarelli

Formerly a Fine Art Major, Rebecca is a pastor's wife and mother of two young children- Bella & Joey! After growing up in Chattanooga, Tennessee, Rebecca and her family now reside in Fort Worth, Texas. She is involved in helping women in crisis with a women's ministry group called Journey of Sisters, as she continues to have a passion for art and sharing the love of Jesus. www.JourneyofSisters.com

www.ingramcontent.com/pod-product-compliance
Lightning Source LLC
Chambersburg PA
CBHW041231040426
42444CB00002B/129